CONTENTS

YOU ARE ENOUGH:
Keeping It 100 With Yourself 2.0

Lisa Wright Bryant, M.Th.

Published by:

LM Bryant Consulting, LLC
Claymont De 19703
www.bryconsult.com

Cover by D. Joseph Bryant & Nicolas J. Bryant
Editor: D. Joseph Bryant

BOOKING REQUESTS

For booking requests for:

Lisa Wright Bryant

LM Bryant Consulting, LLC

Contact Jennifer Henry info@bryconsult.com

www.bryconsult.com 877-737-9719

BOOK DEDICATION:

Heavenly Father, how You have blessed me. Everything I dreamed about as a child, you gave me. Thank You for sparing my life, strengthening me, making me free and empowering me to empower others.

To my husband, Pup, who is THEE most patient man on earth. You sho nuff have your hands full with me! Thank you for your guidance, your coaching, your support, your covering but most importantly, your love!! 8888

To my Natalie & Nicolas, thanks for letting me use you to be my sounding board while writing this book. Love y'all to life!

To my Teri. Thank you for letting me be your Momma Lisa! I love you so much!

To my Mommy, G Money (Geri Wright) if it wasn't for your sacrifices, I would have never fulfilled my dreams. I love you more than you know.

To My Poppi, thank you for loving me enough to bless someone else with me. Love you forever!

To My Daddy, thank for accepting the blessing called ME! Love you forever!

To Mom Elva & Mom JoAnn, thank you for your love and support in everything I do! I love you!

To the best Godmother, I love you Ms. Naomi.

To My Goddaughter Ashli, I am so proud of you. I couldn't love you anymore than if you were my own daughter! Follow your dreams!!

Love to my Godbrothers and Godsisters, the late Renee, Gary, Darryl aka "6-9, and Kimmy! Y'all are my peoples!

To my siblings, Carl, Fatima, Kerry, Linda, Tammy, Chris, Mariam,

Dwight, Tanita, Pat, Kevin, Sean, Crissy, I love you all sooo much!!

To my Best Friend Charity, "God has been so good to me, he opened doors I could not see". Did we really know what that meant at 18 years old? Thank you for being my "ride and live" BFF! Love you girl!

To my sister girls/my friends thank you for your friendship. Love y'all!!!

To my Theta Lambda & Epsilon Omega Zeta Chapters of Zeta Phi Beta Sorority, Inc., you all don't even know what you mean to me! So proud of you all! SZL

To DLM, see yall at our Sunday Brunch!

To Donna Duffy and Lois Hoffman who encouraged me to write this book. Donna, thank you for showing me it's okay to be true to yourself in business despite the twists and turns, just trust in my God! Lois thanks for believing in me and steering me in the right direction!

To Kirk Franklin, thank you for being so transparent in your music and for you being so dope! Your music played constantly while I was writing this book. TEARS! REJOICING! TEARS!

To the awesome consultants of LM Bryant Consulting, LLC! Man, Y'all are truly my ride and live peoples!

To every college and university that has allowed or will allow me to empower their students. Thank you!

Lastly, this is dedicated to 13-year-old Lisa Michele Wright. You thought you were the ugliest, silliest preteen who dreamed that you would grow up to be beautiful, attend West Chester State College, become a teacher, be loved by an awesome husband and have loving and caring children. Although your perception of yourself was so very off, your dreams were not. They came true!!! Just know that you are enough.

"WHY, YOU ARE ENOUGH: KEEPING IT 100 WITH YOURSELF 2.0"

I know many of you are asking that question. Some may say I should write another book to continue the story. I hear what you are saying. However, I have realized there are more details that must be included to this story that could not be separated by another book. Because of that, I dedicated more attention to fear and courage. In my discussions with our readers, I have found that many of them struggle with those areas which has prevented them from really embracing that they are enough. So, I know if they are struggling, there are many more that are.

Lisa, why Is the book cover blurry?

The cover is intentionally blurred because it represents a time when what I saw was distorted. I continually looked at myself with a myopic lens until I realized that I was enough! So, for the ones that have read the book before, buckle up. For the ones that have not, you really have to buckle up! What was in the first book was only half of the journey! *Lisa Wright Bryant*

FOREWORD:

2 Corinthians 12:9 KJVS [9] And he said unto me, My grace is sufficient for thee: for my strength is made perfect in weakness. Most gladly therefore will I rather glory in my infirmities, that the power of Christ may rest upon me.

In the almost 20 years that my wife and I have known Lisa, she has been transparent. It has been in her transparency that she has served as an example of the power of God in the life of a believer. Through her transparency, one could clearly see that she was experiencing a particular hardship.

Yet, though she acknowledged the reality of her experience, it was also apparent that she didn't waver in her believing God for the victory. There is circumstance and there is the formulation of character. Lisa has synchronized the two.

I have several mottos that I've developed over the years. One of which is "All that call upon the name of the Lord shall be saved". Another is "God is God of the impossible. Allow him a chance to be God of the impossible in your life".

After reading the introduction of her new book, having the privilege of attending theology school with her and sharing a small part of her life's journey, I am eagerly looking forward to reading her book in its entirety. What has always been true of Lisa and her husband is that they are concerned with the welfare of others. So I am excited about her sharing to help others in their life's journey as they either come to live by faith or grow in the grace and knowledge of the Lord. Nathaniel McCollum, Th.D.

I first met Lisa when we were both seventeen. We were both young and naïve about life and the purpose that God ultimately had for us. A part of His plan was that Lisa and I were to become best friends. Through ups and downs in this life's journey, we have each had a front row seat to watch the growth of another. There seemed to be so much to be fearful about on this journey. We supported each other through prayer, scripture, and laughter. It was always enough. What a blessing it has been to support and be supported by your best friend.

I have watched Lisa grow into a phenomenal woman of God, who does not take her calling lightly. She lives with an everyday purpose to guide all within her reach to the light of Christ and to illuminate the golden character that can reside within us all. This book is a timely complement to everyday life. So often in society, there is a grand self-deception that fear is normal, that change is not necessary, or that life does not involve risk. None of those things are true. In a time when the world is seemingly content to embrace nonsense as reality, there is a need for a voice in the wilderness to awaken the senses and steer those who are willing to listen, back to the truth of self-purpose.

Through pain and process, Lisa has learned the importance of keeping it real with oneself. She has realized, as we all should, that lives are meant to be lived, experiences are meant to be shared, and growth is meant to be testified about. Her words are guaranteed to change your position on your place in the world, if you are willing and open. This book was written with a fervent desire that all would begin to see their purpose and find the inner determination to make the change necessary to walk completely in it. Please read this offering by this amazing woman who is willing to share her weakness, so that you can find your strength. It is indeed a joy and an honor to call her my friend. Charity Jones

When I first met Lisa, it was because she almost always stood in front of me at the church we both attended. I had to have someone ask her to move, as our director was "height challenged!" This went on for several years, with us just "seeing" each other from a distance. I never saw her with anyone except this one guy from time to time, who turned out to be her brother. One day, I asked a mutual friend about her and was promptly told: "not to even bother." I moved on as I didn't want to create an issue for her in our circle.

Later on, I invited her to sing background for me at a concert I was scheduled to do, and she accepted. That was the first of many dates. After 3 major breakups and the routine challenges couples go through, we tied the knot, jumped the broom, etc...

For the last twenty-some years, I have watched Lisa go through many trials and tribulations. I've seen ups and downs, ins and outs, and even sideways maneuvers. But the thing that has inspired me the most is her ability to rebound. Even when things looked cwaazzee (yes, that's how I spelled it because that's how it was!), she managed to keep on a-smilin'. She may have been broken inside, but she kept up a good look for the people around her, myself included.

Dealing with problems when you, yourself are an issue, takes a great deal of courage. And though she would tell you that at times she was less than courageous, that's a far cry from the truth. From learning that I had another child (from a relationship I had prior to our meeting – don't throw me under the bus! LOL) while she was pregnant with our son, Nico, to finding that our own daughter had special needs, to a seventeen-month illness, the road has not been easy. But I'm glad to say that she is still here and kicking and helping others in the process!

So, to the love of my life, congratulations are in order on this, the first of many compositions that have a singular purpose – helping others overcome similar problems and walking in His Divine Liberty and in what He made them to be. Love always & 4-ever! Pup

INTRODUCTION

"Lynnette, guess what? I am writing a book about being true to yourself and embracing who you are!" "Lisa, you are the right person to write it because you have the experience of not knowing who you are."

That was a conversation I had with one of my sorors at our chapter's 35th anniversary. And she was right. I do have the experience of not knowing AND embracing who I am. As a teenager, I tried to fit in because the Lisa I saw in the mirror was not pretty enough and not popular enough to get a boyfriend. As a young adult, inadequacy, and insecurity were replaced by becoming an overachiever and perfectionist that led me to have a short-lived marriage, which left me with low self-esteem.

But one day, I realized that the very conversations I was having with myself were a bunch of lies. Instead of being the person that tried to please everybody, who tried to fit in and be who everyone else wanted me to be, with God's help, I made the decision to be the Lisa the Lord created me to be. I decided that I would no longer try to fit into the mold that others formed for me. I would instead be the role model for others to chart their own course and accept that sometimes it would go against the grain. That decision has not been easy for me nor has it been without backslides and setbacks. It has caused an inner turmoil that many times I have wished would go away. But instead of wishing it would leave, I suited up for the fight of my life. Sometimes fighting standing, sometimes fighting laying down, sometimes fighting on my knees. But nevertheless, I have fought with a winning mentality.

This book has been a journey for me. I didn't want to write it. I didn't want to be so transparent because there are some things that will be revealed about me that I was not ready for everyone to know. I wasn't ready for the judgments and the prying eyes into my personal life. But I realize it is not what I want. Not if I am going to empower you to let go. Another reason I didn't want to write this book was, though I am an extrovert in most situations, over the years, I have become a closet introvert because of past persecutions and betrayals which caused me to create Fort Knox type walls around my heart. This has caused me to show the likeable, friendly, gregarious Lisa who strives to make sure everyone is comfortable and enjoying themselves. All the while, the flawed and insecure Lisa has operated in fear, wondering when will that person find out that I am just as nervous and fearful as they are.

You see, I have struggled for years with the two Lisas. This was evident for the entire state of Delaware and parts of N.J. and Delaware County to see when my husband DJ & I hosted "Gospel Live with DJ & Lisa" for several years on Channel 28. When our Executive Producer, Tim Qualls said, "the entire State of Delaware was watching", the struggle of what Lisa should I show became front and center for everyone around me to watch. Even my husband was thrown off. For the first 3 shows, I froze and became mechanical in my delivery because I didn't know which Lisa to show. Later, with the help of God, I was delivered from that and the show went on for almost 2 years with me hosting it and having fun.

The real, for real reason I tried to stop writing this book is because I didn't want to face the ugly truth about myself. I knew I was enough and I was good with that. But I was not ready to be 100% with myself concerning past mistakes and missteps. You know we don't like seeing our flawed self. We don't like to see when our actions or circumstances are less than perfect. We don't like to be viewed in a negative light. This book has caused me to remember some things in my life that I didn't want to relive. Emotions that I thought I had faced and dealt with, I now realized I had not. People that I thought I had forgiven, I realized that I had not. This book has helped me to face past hurts, situations, and emotions and to move on.

So, I had to write this book - for you. I had to let you know that you are greater than the lies you tell yourself. I had to tell you that it's not always going to be this way. I had to let you know that it is time to let go of the ugliness that you have held close and carried for so long. I had to tell you that no matter what you have been through or are going through, you will get through it! I had to tell you that you are enough. You just have to keep it 100 with yourself. *"To thine own self be true, and it must follow, as the night the day, thou canst not then be false to any man." William Shakespeare [1] "As I have said, the first thing is to be honest with yourself. You can never have an impact on society if you have not changed yourself... Great peacemakers are all people of integrity, of honesty, but humility." Nelson Mandela[2]*

What Are Your Thoughts About the Journey You Are About to Take?

Do you know of anything that would stop you from taking this journey? If so, what is it?

Date: ____

CHAPTER ONE:

"THE DEADLY EFFECTS OF EXTERNAL FORCES"

The Media

You may say, "Lisa, the title of this chapter is SO dramatic!" What do you mean, "the deadly effects"? The external forces are not going to kill you!!!" I beg to differ. Haven't you heard the saying, "you are a product of your environment? Or nothing good can come out of THAT neighborhood because of (fill in the blanks) or you may hear, tired of being a B cup? Call 1-888-big-boob to have breasts like this model that everyone wants to look like". Before you know it, you will begin to internalize it, believe it and act like it. The media is one of the sources that can convince you that you are not enough.

If you are constantly fed through the media (and we are) that you must look flawless, all THE time, then you will eventually begin to believe that you must look like you just stepped off a runway, which can totally become a head game. Yes, I have found myself watching the television and seeing ladies whose arms are buffed. And I look at my arms and see that they are the opposite of buffed. Personally, it has taken me a minute to get to the point that the subliminal message of perfection is not one that I must adhere to. I had to realize that as long as I am working on me by working out and eating healthy, I'm good! So, if you find yourself believing the flimflam of the media, you'd better act like Public Enemy and tell yourself, "don't believe the hype!"

So, speaking of the media, one of the deadly effects that can convince us that we are not enough is looking at airbrushed celebrity photos in awe and marveling at the perfection. In the article "The Truth About Advertisements and Airbrushing" that was published in the online magazine Chron, it says, *"Airbrushing involves retouching photos to remove flaws or change or enhance the image. In the days before digital media, airbrushing involved painting with an airbrush. Today, computer programs such as Photoshop allow for almost endless manipulation of images. Some companies have come under fire for airbrushing the images of models and other celebrities into unrealistic portrayals of "perfect" women."* [3] Wait a minute! Four words jump out at me. "Remove, Change, Enhance and Manipulation". Oh, it gets even worse. According to an article on telegraph.co.uk, men are being affected by the altered images that are the final results of airbrushing. *"Pictures that exaggerate models' muscle development and definition can encourage "unhealthy muscle-enhancing behaviours" such as taking steroids or other supplements)" It goes on to say that experts have concluded, "boys and men can also suffer depression, anxiety, sexual dissatisfaction, and low self-esteem."* [4] Even though studies don't state death as a side effect, it is. There is a death in your spirit. Your joy light is snuffed out because you start believing the lie.

The stereotypical lie doesn't stop with the magazines and the TV but has even been a part of our childhood toys. When I was a little girl, I wanted the white doll baby with long blonde hair and blue eyes. I didn't want the black doll baby because the black doll baby was ugly with ugly hair. The message I, along with so many other little sister girls was, "you are pretty when you have long hair". So that's what I prayed for. I would put a pillowcase on my head and pretend that it was my long, flowing hair. Thank God that some toy makers now make dolls of various ethnicities but unfortunately, the damage has been done to the previous generations.

Your Circle of Friends

Another deadly external force can be surrounding yourself with a group of so-called, toxic friends. First of all, do you really believe they are "your friends"? Keep it 100 with yourself. You know you can't trust 85% of them, but because you don't want to be alone, you keep those ratchet and lecherous friends around you. You are doing yourself more harm than good. You are better off spending time alone than with people who do not celebrate your existence. You must be conscious of the role you have allowed these people to play in your life. These life-sucking people that are in your inner circle are feeding you a constant diet of negativity and I can guarantee you they are not supporting or encouraging you to be your best self. In fact, they are probably encouraging you to be just as self-degrading as they are, if not more. Or those people are smiling in your face, expressing their love and loyalty to you, all the while betraying you behind your back. It's like they are hugging you with one hand and stabbing you in the back with the other. Been there.

There was a young lady that I used to work with that I knew was a treacherous gossiper. When I started with the company, we worked in two different departments. I had heard some things about her and her tendency to run her mouth. She barely spoke to me and I was okay with that. Then I was transferred to her department and we became co-workers. During this time of transition, I was planning my wedding and I shared my plans and my excitement with her. You see, when I get excited I bubble (thanks for the term Nanny!). I feel when I am happy, I want others to rejoice with me. Little did I know there was no rejoicing and this young lady was telling everyone everything I shared with her. It was not until one of my mentors/co-workers pulled me aside and told me to stop telling her things. I was devastated and angry at myself. I felt stupid and betrayed. It wasn't that I didn't see the signs. I simply chose to ignore them because this young lady had now become my "friend". So, you not only want to be careful who is in your circle, you also want to heed the warning signs if and when they appear.

There are many of you that have haters in your circle. People who are so covetous of you that they emit a green hue of envy every time they are around you. They even come off like they care about you, except they talk down to you to depreciate you.

But in actuality, they are jealous of you. According to dictionary.com the word "jealous" is defined as *"feeling resentment against someone because of that person's rivalry, success, or advantages....*[5] Heidi Klum said, *"I think it's important to get your surroundings as well as yourself into a positive state - meaning surround yourself with positive people, not the kind who are negative and jealous of everything you do"*. [6] Those negative forces and the seeds that they plant in your spirit can utterly destroy you. Those seeds can suggest that you are less than enough. And by you co-signing with those loud voices in your ear, you begin to operate like an imposter, a shell of your true self. How in the world can you live out the purpose that God laid out for you if you are as phony as Michael Jackson's nose? Those around you that operate in jealousy are subconsciously tearing you down! Guess what? If you believe it, it will destroy you! Then, those jealous so-called "friends" will point out your flaws and exploit them for all the world to see. You have to ask yourself, why do you keep them around? Why are you ignoring the caution signs telling you that those so-called friends are literally sucking the life out of you? Why are you tolerating those "frienemies" belittling you and talking down to you, all under the pretense of "keeping it real"? No hun, it's time for you to keep it 100 with yourself and do some friendship circle spring cleaning. If you want to grow, those poisonous vipers have to go!

Family and Childhood Events

My God, this is a biggie! According to vocabulary.com, the word, "formative", *"is a word that describes something that made you who you are. You might call your adolescence your formative years because that time period had such a strong influence on the rest of your life."* [7] Ah yes, the formative years. The time of your life that you were the most impressionable. The time when you knew what foods you did or did not like. The time when others knew whether you were quiet or a talker. The time when you were curious about the world and was inquisitive enough to ask about it. However, it was also the time when positive and negative seeds were planted and depending on which ones were watered, are now ripe for harvesting.

What do I mean? If you were taught to be kind and loving to others as a child, chances are, you are kind and loving now. If you were taught to be mean and abusive as a child, chances are, you are mean and abusive now. Now here's the thing. I know you had no control over how you were raised and what standards and morals were instilled in you as a child. However, as an adult, you still have the choice to say, "I'm not following the path that was set before me. I choose to choose differently". Or you can say, "if it was good for my family, it is good enough for me." If you choose to go contrary to your negative teachings, it might be too difficult for you to tackle on your own. Don't be ashamed to enlist help from positive friends, a minister or seek professional help. Whatever you do, you must uproot those damaging seeds that have turned into weeds when they were planted in your spirit. Those seeds can have a lifelong effect on you, especially if you were a victim of child abuse.

According to psychologytoday.com, (things related to) "child abuse" are likely to conjure up horror stories that appear from time to time – physical beatings, a child locked in a closet or tied up for long periods; or the unimaginable – like Ariel Castro's imprisonment of young girls. But in fact, abuse takes many forms, beyond the physical. Recent research finds that its impact is long lasting. It extends far into adulthood, where it affects both physical and mental health. As Faulkner wrote, *"The past is never dead. It's not even past."*[8]

When I was 7 years old, I was molested by my baby sitter's adult nephew. My parents were separated at the time and my mother worked various shifts at the hospital. So, the babysitter across the street would watch my 2-year-old brother and me until she got home from work. Our babysitter was an elderly woman and many times would sit us in front of the television and fall asleep. Her husband and brother in law would look out for my brother and me and a couple of the other kids in the neighborhood that she watched when she fell asleep.

One day, the nephew came to stay. He seemed okay. He watched wrestling and wore some things with the Marines emblem on it. One evening, he asked me to come upstairs. The babysitter was sleep, and my brother and I were watching television at the time. So, I followed him. He then proceeded to lift my dress, pull my underwear down and perform oral sex on me. I didn't know what was going on. But my first instinct was to protect my brother. When my Mom picked us up that night, I didn't tell her anything. In fact, like many children do, I kept it a secret for many years. When I finally revealed it to her, of course, it was too late for her to press charges. The babysitter had died and the nephew was long gone. But it wasn't too late for the effects of the abuse to take root in my spirit.

In retrospect, throughout my life, I battled the effects of the abuse. I felt shame. I felt guilty. Why did I go upstairs? I felt an overwhelming need to protect my brother. I felt like a victim. I became a people pleaser because in my mind if the person was happy with me, they wouldn't hurt me. I felt that there was something wrong with me because if there wasn't, that man would not have touched me. I even felt like my parents didn't protect me like I felt they should have. I was angry at the babysitter because she was right there and she could not protect me from her family member. All of those emotions PLAGUED me for decades. It wasn't until my late 40s that I talked to my husband, asking him to pray for me. I asked God to deliver me from the hate for this man AND the babysitter, the resentment I felt towards my family and the undue burden of being a savior to my now adult brother. I sought the Lord for deliverance from internalizing things because my thought was, "no one would do anything, just like they didn't when I was 7, so why should I speak up"? It wasn't until I realized over the last few years that this action was affecting every area of my life.

I blamed myself, even more when I realized that my son's

middle name was the same as the man who molested me. HOW COULD I BE SO STUPID????? It didn't matter that my son's middle name was his father's. No, I just couldn't believe that I could be such a fool to make such a grave mistake. Yet again, I wasn't enough. I wasn't strong enough to say, "ummm Pup, no let's pick a different name". I BEAT MYSELF UP!!! I wasn't being my best self. I was going through life with a beautiful mask on, instead of allowing the world to see the real Lisa Michele. It was then that I made up my mind that I would no longer be a victim but walk in the victory that I had all along. I decided that I would no longer hurt to avoid addressing problems. It was then that I decided that I had to start keeping it 100 with myself and not care who didn't like it.

Peer Pressure

Many of us think that peer pressure only occurs during childhood. Really? Unfortunately, that is so far from the truth. According to Wikipedia.com, "peer pressure" is defined as, " *the direct influence on people by peers, or an individual who gets encouraged to follow their peers by changing their attitudes, values, or behaviors to conform to those of the influencing group or individual. This type of pressure differs from general social pressure because it causes an individual to change in response to a feeling of being pressured or influenced from a peer or peer group.*" [9] Nowhere is the definition limited to children under the age of 21. Peer pressure is real! Many people become a chameleon so they can fit into an organization, club or a clique. This pressure can also cause you to do things that you said you would never do. Things that you were raised to know better. If you are not careful, peer pressure will take you down a road that will cause you to ask, "how did I get here?"

So how do you not fall into the trap of peer pressure? I mean really, how do you not give into the temptation of going with the crowd and not against the grain? The answer is simple but complex. First, you must know why you believe what you believe. For example, if you believe smoking marijuana is wrong, you must know WHY you believe it is wrong? The answer is NOT "because my mom said it would fry my brain cells" or "because someone told me it was not good." No, the answer must be an answer that comes from you. An answer that is a conviction that, although you are challenged, you won't give in to it because it is your belief that smoking marijuana is not right for you. So, if peer pressure knocks on your door regarding smoking marijuana or doing anything that you know that you know that you know is not right for you, you can resist the temptation and as the Good Book says, "it will flee from you". Those people who are trying to make you cave in will eventually leave you alone when they see that the pressure is falling on deaf ears.

Intimidation

According to Wikipedia, the definition of "*intimidation*" is, "*intentional behavior that "would cause a person of ordinary sensibilities to fear injury or harm.*" It is not necessary to prove that the behavior was so violent as to cause terror or that the victim was actually frightened. Unfortunately, in today's society, there is so much that can cause intimidation in us. What we see or hear on our Twitter feed or on the news or a blog can be intimidating. Or your boss on your new job or your new teacher/professor can be intimidating. The very thought of those situations can invoke a paralyzing fear that can cause you to go from a confident and carefree individual to a spineless and fearful shadow of your true self.

It's one thing to be intimidated by a situation. You must face that situation head-on and be fearless about conquering that new situation. You know you can do it. You've done it countless times before. But to many of you, it's something different to be intimidated by a person, especially someone who wants to intentionally do so. Those people whose goal in life is to intimidate you and to create you in their image are driven by fear. Fear that you are better than them. Fear that you will succeed and exceed greater than them. Fear that you will get more "shine" than them. Fear that you will walk away from them and be okay. Fear that you will...be okay without them. Well, guess what? Just like you conquered that intimidating situation, you can do the same in dealing with that intimidating person, even if it means that you must excommunicate them from your life. No one, I repeat, no one is worth having in your life if their primary mission is to intimidate you out of being your true selves.

But you may ask, “how do I do that”? “How do I stop allowing myself to be intimidated?” I am going to be honest with you. It will take much time and prayer. It may even take a visit to your minister or a professional to help you. Depending on the level of the intimidation, you may have to involve the authorities. But you will have to separate yourself from the person, especially if it has been going on for a long period of time. Whatever the choice, you must decide that you will no longer allow someone to manipulate you into thinking that their image of you is less than who you are.

Another and even better way to even avoid intimidation is to know your worth. When you know your value, your worth, there is no one who can tell you different. It’s just like someone who works a 9-5 every day, pays bills and has to take care of themselves, approaching Queen Elizabeth and telling her that she wasn’t nothing, not going to be nothing and was stupid. That’s a funny visual, isn’t it? Well, the same with us. When you know that you are a king, a queen and have so much to offer the world, nothing, I repeat, nothing that anyone says to you about you is going to stick. You are not going to believe the foolish rhetoric that people may try to tear you down with because you know who you are. You won’t accept someone else’s definition of “You”, but instead, you will allow it to roll off of you like water rolls off of duck feathers.

So, remember that intimidators are cowards and bullies who operate in fear! Fear that you are better than them, will accomplish more than them, and maybe more liked than them. You don’t have to accept that foolishness. You are more than enough. *“Intimidation is meant to override our own sense of self worth. It only works if we allow it to affect us and then act out of fear to please". Shannon Thomas* [10]

WHAT ARE YOUR THOUGHTS?

What deadly forces can you eliminate from your environment?

Do you want to eliminate those influences?

If not, why not?

If so, who will you enlist to assist you in making the changes?

CHAPTER TWO:

THE DEADLY EFFECTS OF THE INTERNAL STRUGGLES

"I can't give you a sure-fire formula for success, but I can give you a formula for failure: try to please everybody all the time." Herbert Bayard Swope [11]

This chapter has been a great challenge for me. From struggling with why my biological father didn't want me, to trying to fit in with cliques at school, trying to figure out why my ex-husband didn't want me, even feeling and sometimes struggling with acceptance and rejection within my own household. Does that resonate with any of you? You may be able to relate to all or some of the scenarios. Maybe none of them. It doesn't matter whether or not I have mentioned your situation because at the end of the day if you struggle with any scenario of acceptance and rejection, today is the day to face those situations head on. Yes, you want to evict it from your life but before you do, for some of you, it's time to stop denying it, acknowledge it and get help in overcoming it. I can guarantee you that it is stopping you from living in your best self.

I started this chapter talking about situations that I have faced in this area. Challenges that began to come to the surface when I started writing this book. See I, like many of you, thought I had dealt with this area in my life. But I found out that I had simply pushed those issues into a sub-basement closet and threw away the key. Or so I thought.

But one thing I have discovered about suppressed, unresolved issues; they come back to haunt you. They trickle, they leak, or they come back in a deluge. For me, it's been a slow leak. You know what I mean? The kind that not only slowly flows but in the quiet of the night, it makes a sound. Like a faucet that you try to turn off but because it is broken, it continues to flow. If that leak is not fixed, it will leave you with a huge water bill.

The issues of acceptance and rejection that I faced started in a situation in which I had no say in the matter. My biological father was a teenager who by the time he was 21, had 3 children, 2 with his wife, 1 with my mom. I was his firstborn. My young parents did not get married at the time which caused my mom to raise me on her own, with my grandmother's help. My father went on to marry my brothers and my sisters' mom, my beloved stepmother #1. (RIP Mom Sissie). My mom went on with her life and rekindled a friendship and later married my daddy. My mom and my daddy, who is not my biological father, had a conversation about him adopting me. He agreed, and the rest is history. But, in order for Daddy to adopt me, my Poppi (my biological father), had to sign papers to grant the adoption, thus signing away his parental rights. Here's the thing. I COULD NOT ASK FOR A BETTER DADDY! If you didn't know that he wasn't my biological father prior to this book, you would not have known the truth.

My daddy has always loved me as if he sired me himself. My struggle was why didn't my biological father want me? Why was I the only one given away? Why was I the only one that had a different last name? Why didn't some of the relatives on that side of the family know that I even existed? I tell you, I was sooo jacked up. I then became a people pleaser because if I was "good enough", then my father would not have given me away. If I was perfect in every way, I would be accepted. He and I later had a conversation about the past. Poppi shared that he felt that Daddy could give me a better life. He felt that he was doing what was best for me. As an adult, I can understand that. But as a child, I was damaged. This has caused me to live most of my life with a layered mask. The thought that if I showed you my real self, my true self, then you would not accept me, thus rejecting me. This has caused great pain not only for me but for the people closest to me.

That feeling of rejection was intensified when I went through a divorce at the age of 25. I thought that when I got married, it would be forever. Even though I saw the warning signs, I ignored them. I was determined that I could be everything that my ex-husband needed so he would not leave me like most of the men had previously done. I believed if anything went to the left, I had the power in the situation and I could keep him. It took me years and figurative bumps on the head to understand that you only have the power to change yourself.

When the marriage dissolved, not only was I devastated but I was depressed. I was so depressed, disappointed in myself and embarrassed that I begin to take the prescription drug, Xanax, to help me cope with all the guilt that I carried like it was my pocketbook. I felt like once again, another person I loved rejected me. But in essence, it wasn't that he rejected me, the fact is we were not meant to be together.

Back then, I thought if I was just (whatever the word of the day was) then my marriage would not have failed. I believed I wasn't enough woman for my ex-husband. If I could just be someone else or do something else, then he would not reject me. You must remember that the burden of being accepted or rejected does not fall on you. You don't have to do stupid pet tricks to get someone to accept you. You don't have to live this life in fear of being rejected because you are not perceived to be...

So, if you are reading this book, then you can relate to my story. Unfortunately, acceptance and rejection have become more prevalent in our society. From acceptance to jobs to membership in organizations to how many likes you get on Instagram. Yup, it has become a big part of our lives. The problem comes in when our desire for acceptance becomes a driving and blinding force that causes us to become a chameleon, steeped in fear of being our true selves. The issue is when even the very thought of rejection sends you into a downward spiral, causing you to go to your proverbial dresser drawer to get your best mask.

On the flip side, not accepting yourself and who you are is just as detrimental as chasing someone's acceptance. You are hard on yourself and you beat yourself up because you made a mistake or you are not pretty enough or not smart enough or you just feel like you are not enough. Thus, the title of this book! It's time out for lack of acceptance of yourself! When you live your life, no wait let me rephrase that, when you exist in life with those flawed, superhero lenses on, you are living a lie. When you exist (notice I said exist) as a perfectionist, the moment you fail a test, or lose your Visa card, or write down the wrong number for your organization's report, you begin to go toe-to-toe with yourself. It's like, "in this corner, you have (insert your name), from (your hometown), weighing in at (your weight) and in this corner, you have (insert your name), from (your hometown), weighing in at (your weight). You are fighting yourself. You are whipping your own tail because YOU refuse to accept your imperfections, your flaws, your mistakes. And because you are so afraid of making mistakes, you turn down many prospects that can lead to even greater opportunities. Can I tell you something? It's time to let that go! There is growth in mistakes, a stretching in perceived failures. So, I have a question for you. How can others accept you when you refuse to accept yourself?

Do you find yourself in the "rejection and acceptance" trap over and over again? Are you in a relationship whose foundation is built on "please accept me and don't reject me"? Or are you simply tired of being hurt, running behind people who accept a shadow of yourself? What do you do? I mean really. What do you do? I'm going to tell you, real talk, number 1, prayer changes everything. Many of you are so deep in that thing, that only prayer can get you out of that trap. Another option is one that you will constantly "hear" me refer to. Seek help from a professional. There is nothing wrong with sitting down with a licensed counselor who can help you to get to the root of the need for the acceptance trap.

But what you must remember is you should not strive to be accepted by others but make a promise to yourself to accept yourself. If people don't accept the real you, guess what? You don't need them. Remember, you must remember that you are enough and you don't need the acceptance of others to convince you otherwise.

WHAT ARE YOUR THOUGHTS?

Are you fighting to be accepted?

If yes, why?

What are your thoughts about acceptance and rejections?

CHAPTER THREE:

OVERCOMING PEOPLE'S OPINIONS

"Your time is limited, so don't waste it living someone else's life. Don't be trapped by dogma-which is living with the results of other people's thinking. Don't let the noise of others' opinions drown out your own inner voice. And most important, have the courage to follow your heart and intuition." Steve Jobs [12]

This chapter serves as a continuation of the preceding chapter's topic of "Acceptance & Rejection". Let me tell you. Living your life according to the opinions of other people will definitely cause you much confusion. Now, people pleasers will do anything to delight someone at their own expense. People who are more concerned about other people's opinions, simply don't have or don't trust their own opinions. For example, you made the decision to eat healthy and have committed yourself to do so.

One evening, you go out to dinner with some friends and decide to order a slice of chocolate cake as a reward for all your hard work. But then, you decide against it because you don't want to hear the opinions and comments of your friends. You decide to get a bowl of fruit instead. Your friends never indicated that they would make comments. How could they? They are not mind readers so they didn't know that you were going to order a dessert! But you just assumed that they would make negative comments and in your mind, you are not up to it. Ugh! But what makes matters worse is this type of mindset can paralyze you and cause you not to move forward because of the opinions of others, which by the way is a form of fear. Don't let those anticipated and fake opinions stop you from doing what you want to do. You'd better eat that cake, Anna Mae! [13]

Do you see how you can let someone's opinions or assumed opinions guide your decisions? But my question is, why do you think someone else's opinion is more valuable than your own? I mean really, do you think that low of yourself, that you are more like the scarecrow from the Wizard of Oz/the Wiz that wished he had a brain than an adult that can think for themselves? Don't you know that when you value someone else's opinion over your own that you are elevating them to a position that they are not equipped to fill?

Now, I'm not saying that we should not seek a mentor or ask someone for advice or wise counsel from time to time. No. What I'm saying is you are doing yourself a disservice when you make decisions and execute actions based on what someone else feels about the situation. You lose the essence of who you are simply because you don't feel you know enough or are enough to make the decision on your own.

There are three things that occur when you are driven to live your life based on the opinions of others. They are confusion, strife, and resentment. 1 Kings 18:21 NIV says, "*Elijah went before the people and said, "How long will you waver between two opinions? If the LORD is God, follow him; but if Baal is God, follow him." But the people said nothing.*" [14] The statement, "How long will you waver between two opinions" clearly shows confusion. I can just imagine Elijah saying that statement with an attitude. The children of Israel were swinging like a pendulum between two opinions and it sounded like Elijah was tired of watching them swing back and forth. One day they follow God, the next day they follow Baal. Really, can you just stop and make a decision, and stick with it?

There is nothing worse than trying to follow someone who is confused. There is nothing worse than trying to negotiate with someone who is confused. There is nothing worse than being in a relationship with someone that is confused. That confusion comes in because they either don't know what opinion to follow or have gotten too many opinions and don't know which way to turn. As I said before, it's worse trying to follow someone who swings from opinion to opinion to opinion, which can cause confusion to everyone in their circle.

A few years ago, I was a leader of a team with a Multi-Level Marketing company. In my quiet time, I would brainstorm and dream about the direction I wanted to lead my team. I would meet with the team and share my vision and dreams and everyone would be very excited. THEN, I would go to a convention or a large meeting where a successful businessperson who was further up the road than me would be speaking. So, because I felt they knew more I said hey, look at them, and I would change my direction and share that with the team. Then I would go to another convention, I would hear another successful team leader talk about their success and I would think, "well, they said I should do this or that because it worked for them and look at them. They have made it". So, once again, I would do a "course correction" and I would convey the change to our team. Finally, one of the other leaders said, "Lisa! Stop changing your mind. Make a decision and stick with it"! Sheryl Brady, the pastor of The Potter's House of North Dallas, said, "*when your purpose is clear, morale is high, frustration is low, your efforts are concentrated and you attract cooperation.*" [15] The operative phrase is, "*your purpose*". See, when you are wavering from opinion to opinion to opinion, you clearly show that you don't know what your purpose is. If you did, you wouldn't waver between opinions. Let purpose trump confusion!

Strife is another result of being an opinion chaser. I would even say there are two types of strife that come into play: inner and outer strife. When you have inner strife or conflict, that too will affect the people around you. The people you lead, the people in your household, the people you socialize with. When you are constantly chasing opinions, flip-flopping like a fish out of water because you feel that your opinion is not valuable, it causes conflict all around you. The people around you are not sure if what they agreed upon with you on Tuesday, is going to change on Wednesday because of a side meeting you had with someone with an idea different than yours. What this does is uncover your underlying problem, which is a lack of confidence.

The last issue that stems from following other people's opinion is resentment. Again, resentment can be an internal and/or an external issue. Because you lack confidence and you follow everyone's opinion, you can become resentful because you have an opinion that is different than your cloud of witnesses but you are not confident enough to stand up for yourself. Then to compound the issue, if you are in leadership, your team, organization, etc, can become resentful of you because they are saying behind your back, "just make a decision and stick to it!" They resent you because you swing like a pendulum with your decisions. How can you effectively lead if you can't even lead in your thoughts?

So, I have a question for you. What if everyone else is right and you are not? What if you are headed to the left and everyone is on the right road? What do you do? Do you purposely go to the opposite direction of everyone else to prove that you have a mind of your own? Do you retreat into isolation because you are too embarrassed to admit you are wrong? I mean really, what do you do? Guess what? It is better to make a wrong decision that is totally yours than to run "from pillar to post" trying to get everyone else's opinions that may or may not be the right answer.

So, if you are one that just can't seem to make a decision without asking for the opinion of a minimum of 10 people (lol), please make a decision TODAY to stop running around causing confusion, strife, and resentment by being an opinion chaser. I know that sounds hard but you must keep it 100 with yourself. It's one thing to seek wise counsel from a couple of trusted advisors. It's another to run around with people who you have been inadvertently programmed to think for you, to ask them their opinions because you don't like yours! Remember, you are enough! That means your opinion too!

WHAT ARE YOUR THOUGHTS?

Do you struggle with this area? If so, why do you think you are concerned with the opinions of others?

How do you change your mindset about placing importance on the opinions of others?

What are your thoughts about this chapter?

CHAPTER FOUR:

COMPARING YOURSELF WITH OTHERS

"If you compare yourself with others, you may become vain or bitter, for always there will be greater and lesser persons than yourself." Max Ehrmann [16]

Ooooh, this is a big one! I remember when I was a little girl, my best friend's name was Heidi. She had the most adorable dimples. I remember the comments from others about her dimples. Oh, my goodness, I wanted dimples too. I used to go home and suck my cheeks in to get that dimples effect. Sounds funny? Okay, then lets fast forward. How many of you have said, "I wish I had Tierra's complexion or you wish your mustache grew in like Paul's. Really? Don't you realize that you were created to look like you look? Don't you know that after you were born, God broke the mold? Hmmm, no you don't! That's why you are reading this book because you haven't been keeping it 100 with yourself. You compare yourself with other's because you find yourself accentuating your flaws instead of your assets. Let me tell you something. We as a people, want others to accept us for who we are, but we don't accept ourselves because we want to be like someone else.

Comparing ourselves with other people is a trap that comes directly from the enemy of your soul. When you begin to live in the "what's wrong with me" mindset, you begin to elevate others above you, putting them on a pedestal and worshipping them for their perceived perfections. When you compare your looks to someone else, whether they are prettier or more handsome or shapelier or more muscular than you, you are creating a negative side that can become contagious. You begin to emit a signal to others who struggle with that same spirit and before you know it, you become a clique of negative, miserable people that confident people do not want to socialize with.

Now, let me back up a bit. It's one thing to say, "I want to be in great shape like Madison or I want a six-pack like Donte" and you hire a trainer, join a local gym and change the way you eat. You are not comparing yourself but you recognize that there are changes that need to take place to accomplish your health goals. Yes, that's fine. But even with this area, you must be careful. You could be doing the same exercises as "Madison" or "Donte", however, you may not get the same results which can once again, cause you to go to war with yourself, that may lead to self-sabotage. According to an article in Fitstream.com, *"Keep in mind that the people around you with bodies that you admire won't have achieved those results overnight, but with consistent work and building healthy habits that inched them towards their goals day by day. Don't compare your chapter 1 with someone else's chapter 10. Concentrate on daily improvement and ignore the bigger picture for now.*[17]

In my travels, I have heard of another comparison trap that can jack you up. Comparing your accomplishments and knowledge to someone else's. Really? This type of comparison is a trap within a trap. First of all, it's an apple to oranges comparison. Until you walk a mile in someone else's shoes, you don't know what it took for the person to get to where they are now. You don't know the sacrifices that were made, the tears that were shed, the parties and other social events that were missed because that person that you have made an idol chose to pursue opportunities that may or may not have eluded you. If you want to accomplish more in your life, don't do it because you want to be like someone else. Go for it for you and the generations after you.

Now listen. There is no problem when you want a mentor, someone who is accomplishing what you're striving to achieve in your industry. That is a wise move, to seek out someone like that. The problem of comparing yourself and your accomplishments comes into play when you magnify and even worship someone and what they've done while minimizing your achievements, all while putting yourself down. Even if that person is considered a G.O.A.T. (greatest of all time) in their field, you still should not compare where you are and where they are. By doing so, you are subconsciously saying, "I am not enough. I need to be more like (person) and then I will be (you fill in the blank)."

Another danger with that type of mindset is you really DON'T know what type of person you are comparing yourself to. Honestly, you are only comparing yourself to a persona, a personality that you are only allowed to see. Here you are stressing yourself out, comparing yourself to someone who could potentially be worse off than you. What I mean is, you are comparing yourself to someone's business success, but their personal accomplishments are trash, whereas yours are stellar. You feel me? The time and energy you are using to spin your world of comparison could be used to push you forward. I want to leave you with this thought as we conclude this chapter. What is it about you that causes you to compare yourself? What do you feel that you are lacking that motivates you to seek out a human ruler that you can measure yourself against? I mean really, what is it? You and you alone can answer that question. You have to keep it 100 with yourself before YOU can answer that question.

WHAT ARE YOUR THOUGHTS?

Do you often find yourself comparing yourself to others? If so, why?

Explain what you think about you.

What are your thoughts about this chapter?

CHAPTER FIVE:

F.E.A.R.

"F-E-A-R has two meanings: "Forget everything and run" or "face everything and rise" THE CHOICE IS YOURS". Zig Ziglar [18]

False
Evidence
Appearing
Real

I have alluded to this topic throughout this book thus far. It is mentioned in passing and neatly woven into the tapestry of the words in each chapter. Aside from the introduction, the word "fear" is mentioned in this book 18 times up to this point. According to, "biblestudy.org" the number "18" means, "*bondage*"[19]. According to the Oxford Dictionary, the word, *"Bondage" is defined as "the state of being a slave"*[20]. Fear can literally keep you in bondage and stop you from moving forward, can stop you from living, can stop you from thinking clearly and rationally and can just plain stop you!

You may be wondering why I did not include fear in Chapter One, especially since I addressed intimidation. It seems like a natural progression to talk about fear and intimidation at the same time. But that is not the case. Fear and intimidation are two different things and generates from two different sources. According to Wikipedia, "*intimidation*" is defined as, "*intentional behavior that "would cause a person of ordinary sensibilities" to fear injury or harm"*. This is an external force. However, *"fear"* is defined as, "*An unpleasant, often strong, emotion caused by anticipation or awareness of danger*[21]". The problem is when you allow intimidation to cause fear in your life. The type of fear that grips your heart, that paralyzes you, that convinces you that you can't go on, that you can't accomplish the goals that you created for your life, that you simply can't.

See, you will never hear from me that it is okay to be afraid or that you should embrace fear like a fur coat on a cold, winter day. NOOO! What I will tell you is, when you feel fear instead of allowing it to paralyze you, push it aside and do what you want to accomplish anyway. I'm telling you to use that fear as a stepping stool to help you to go where you need to go. Listen, if you have been raised in fear or if fear is inbred in you it will be a challenge. But this is what I know, you can overcome it. It will take a whole lot of positive self-talk but you can overcome it. It may take you talking to your BFF (hey my Chick), but you can do it. You know how I know? Because this was me.

I was so afraid of pursuing certain things. Those of you who know me may look at me and think, "yeah right", not her. Yes, me. It took me years to run for a position on my alma mater's alumni association board of directors. It took me years to put myself out there as a motivational speaker. But guess what, I did it! And it has been successful for me. But even though I look at my accomplishments now, author, book publisher, alumni BOD member and speaker, I've had to come to grips that it took me years to get over how I allowed fear to limit the pursuit of one of my dreams.

One of the many things I wanted to do when I was a little girl was to be a model. I was a nerdy little girl, however, I dreamed of being a beautiful woman that people admired and adored. That dream was conceived after I read Sophia Loren's autobiography. She said the men would watch her walk down the street because of her beauty. I knew then that I wanted to be a beautiful model in addition to being a concert pianist, an actress, and politician! But when I looked in the mirror, all I saw were glasses, a big forehead and a front tooth that was pointed. Instead of hearing how cute I was, I heard, "hey four eyes", "look at your big head" or "why do you have a dog tooth?"

I still had those comments in the back of my mind when I got up the nerve to enroll in the John Robert Powers Modeling School. I not only excelled in the school but I was chosen a top student in my class by my instructor. This meant that I would compete against students from other classes to represent our school in a citywide competition. I was elated. My dream was about to come true. But.....instead of moving forward and preparing for this competition, I became driven by fear and did not compete. I had an opportunity to pursue my dreams in modeling and "chickened out". I was afraid of everything. At the same time, I decided to enter the "Miss USA" pageant". I wrote a letter, sent my picture and hoped for the best. And yes, I was accepted. I just had to find a sponsor. But, instead of walking across the street to talk to the mayor, like my mother suggested, I decided not to pursue it. The Miss USA pageant was so gracious that they sent me another invitation 2 years later to compete. But, by then, I was going through a divorce which deemed me ineligible. I used to wonder where I would have been if I had followed the dream and not given in to fear. When I struggled with money and my situation was not right, in the past, I would often look back and think the what-ifs. But, I realized that where I am is where I am supposed to be.

You see, I allowed fear to dictate my every movement, my every decision, be a lamp unto my feet, a light unto my path. I allowed fear to be in control, to be my captain, my guide. One of the reasons I am writing this book is because I don't want YOU to make the same mistakes I did. I don't want you to allow fear to cause you to avoid following your dreams. I don't want you to allow fear to cause you to settle for a mundane life full of regrets, anger, and remorse over the "what could have been".

Fear is an ugly, wicked emotion that can make you sell your momma, turn your back on your dreams, make you settle for less than you are worth. If you talk to the average person, I mean really talk to them about their past, their hopes and dreams, many will tell you that fear caused them to settle. Instead of working smarter and pursuing that seemingly impossible career goal, they decided to stay put because they were afraid of the unknown. Fearful that if they jumped from what they know to the unknown, they would somehow miss out or be worse off than where they are. This foolish mindset will cause you to look around 30 years from now and ask yourself, "how did I get here?". The answer is fear. First Lady Eleanor Roosevelt, the wife of President Franklin Delano Roosevelt, said, "*You gain strength, courage, and confidence by every experience in which you really stop to look fear in the face. You must do the thing which you think you cannot do.*[22] There must come a time in this life that we must stop being afraid of the unknown, of people's opinions, the "what ifs" and just do it.

Fear will zap your strength and your confidence. Fear is a criminal that will take everything away from you if you allow it, and you will end up with nothing. The end result can cause you to be a shell of a man/woman that is hopeless, lifeless and alone. Worse yet, fear will tell you that you are not enough. Fear will dictate to you what you can and cannot do. Fear will tell you that you are your mistakes, that you are a failure and that you can't accomplish what your heart tells you that you can. Fear tells you that you are not loved, that no one would understand you, that you are too different to be accepted. Fear can convince you to embrace FEAR as your best friend because no one else will be there for you. You must espouse the lyrics of the Kirk Franklin song, "Hello Fear". You must evict fear from your life, end your love affair with it, divorce it. When it comes knocking at your door, and trust me it will, tell it that it is not welcome in your home. You must believe you are stronger than fear. You are a conqueror and bigger and greater than fear. You must tell fear, "it's between me and you, and I'm not going anywhere"!

I know some of you are reading this and saying, "Lisa I am NOT struggling with fear! I see something I want and I go for it"! Well kudos to you and congratulations! But let me tell you this, fear is multifaceted. You may have the drive and the initiative to pursue your goals but, what about that feeling you had when you were told that new management was taking over your company? Or how did you feel when you were told that you were being considered for a promotion? Or better yet, what about that feeling you had when you were told that your favorite professor was no longer going to teach your favorite class? How did you feel? Fear right? Yup, I know. Let's look at three layers of fear. They are fear of the unknown, fear of success/failure and fear of change.

First fear of the unknown. When DJ & I first got engaged, a sister was sckured, not scared, but sckured. Why? Because of my previous marriage and I really didn't know what to expect. I was afraid that history would repeat itself and I would be a childless, two-time divorcee by the time I was 32. But, I loved DJ so much, so I prayed about it and decided to take a chance. Now, after almost 25 years, I have not regretted it for one moment. There are many of you that feel the same way. You would rather stay in a jacked up situation because you say, "I know this situation. I am afraid what's out there." Or I know this job, so why should I pursue another one. Or WORSE YET, "I will stay in this relationship because I know this crazy. I would rather stay with this crazy then find someone who is crazier. The sad part is, when you talk like this, you are really trying to convince yourself that where you are is not that bad and you are okay. THEN, you have your so called friends "co-signing" by agreeing with you and your fearful babble. You know that's foolishness right?

Another layer of fear is fear of success and failure. The fear of success is more common than you think. I have seen people self sabotage just so they will not get a promotion because they are afraid of the responsibility, the pressures and the expectations that come along with the promotion. I have read studies that show that people tend to self sabotage because they feel like an imposter; that they should not go to the next level because what people see is not what people will get. I talk about the "imposter syndrome" a lot because that was my struggle. And for real, for real, keeping it real 100, I find that too, trying to come back. I would self sabotage with my thoughts which in turn would covertly paralyze my thinking and my actions. I believed that if people only knew that I was not as confident and self assured as I portrayed, then they would not hire me or want to promote me.

This situation did not become apparent in me until I was up for a promotion. I didn't feel worthy to go to the next level, even though my accomplishments reflected otherwise. Praise God, I came to realize that I am more than a conqueror and that imposter title simply did not apply to Lisa Michele!

On the other hand, fear of failure can be just as paralyzing. You are SO afraid of failing that you don't even try. What the What is that? Don't you know that YOU ARE the one that's suffering? Get it together! In my humble opinion, this is the crux of so many people's problems and the reason why they feel that they are not enough. So, you failed a test. So what? So you didn't get the promotion. So what! Stop allowing those teachable moments define your entire life!!!! Did you catch that? I said those "TEACHABLE MOMENTS"? Don't you know that perceived failures are merely experiences divinely designed to allow you to learn and grow? Oprah Winfrey said, *"Think like a queen. A queen is not afraid to fail. Failure is another steppingstone to greatness."* [23] For you brothers, just think like a king, I'm sure Oprah wouldn't mind!

Lastly, the fear of change. So, ask yourself, why do you say in your job interviews, "Oh, I'm flexible. I can adapt to change at the drop of a hat" to impress the interviewer. Then on the way home you are ready to cuss someone out because there is a detour on the road that you frequently travel. Shut yo mouth with your inflexible, self deceiving self. Fear of change will cause you to dig your heels in the sand because what you perceive exists on the other side of change.

Fear of change will cause you to stay up at night because you are afraid of perceived negative implications when your reality becomes your past. I'm telling you, it's time to purge yourself of those fears that are robbing you and declare that you will now live a fearless best life! Remember, YOU ARE ENOUGH! It's time to walk in that! Be here for it! Please keep it 100 with yourself!

WHAT ARE YOUR THOUGHTS ABOUT FEAR?

What have you allowed fear to stop you from accomplishing?

Have you always had an issue with fear?

What other levels of fear has plagued you in your life?

How do you plan to overcome them?

What are your thoughts about this chapter?

How can you relate?

CHAPTER SIX:

IT'S WHAT YOU THINK YOU ARE: LOW SELF ESTEEM

"It's not what you are that is holding you back. It's what you think you are not." Anonymous[24]

While preparing for this book, I reviewed many quotes about low self-esteem. I was so surprised that many of the people quoted were celebrities. Many of them stated how they not only struggled with low self-esteem in the past, but a few of them confessed that they still struggled with it. Some still embraced it. As a person who has this emotion constantly trying to move back in, I disagree. I simply refused to embrace it or welcome it back into my intimate space. In line with the title of this book by keeping it 100 with myself, I have had the proverbial, "1-night stand" with low self-esteem but I refused to remarry it. I simply refuse to allow it to dictate my life and chart my destiny anymore.

So, before I go on, let's look at the true definition of "low self-esteem". According to the UC Davis Health, *"Low self-esteem is a debilitating condition that keeps individuals from realizing their full potential. A person with low self-esteem feels unworthy, incapable, and incompetent. In fact, because the person with low self-esteem feels so poorly about him or herself, these feelings may actually cause the person's continued low self-esteem.*
Here are some signs of low self-esteem: •Negative view of life •Perfectionist attitude •Mistrusting others – even those who show signs of affection •Blaming behavior •Fear of taking risks •Feelings of being unloved and unlovable •Dependence – letting others make decisions •Fear of being ridiculed[25]" I didn't realize that I displayed many of these signs which betrayed me even when I was trying to act as if

I had all the esteem in the world. There are quite a few signs mentioned above but there are a few that we need to take a closer look at. Having a negative outlook on life is a sho 'nuff, sho 'nuff, detriment to your life and the ones around you. Charles F. Glassman, wrote in, "Brain Drain the Breakthrough That Will Change Your Life", *"Believing in negative thoughts is the single greatest obstruction to success."*[26] When you feel as though nothing can go your way no matter what you do, there's an issue. The issue is not your situation or circumstances, the issue is you. You have that "woe is me" attitude and feel nothing good will ever happen to you. As the quote says, that stinking thinking will stop you from achieving success.

What is success? Success is doing what God has created you to do. If He created you to be a businessperson and you are in business, then you are successful. Don't base your level of success on someone else's definition of success. That will trip you up every time. Trust me. I know that too, but that's another book. The negative thinking that you have displayed is a product of low self-esteem. That low self-esteem tells you that all the good that people tell you will happen, will not happen. Low self-esteem tells you that you will never be happy, you will die alone and you will die young, penniless and homeless.

Now, I know the ones that don't suffer from this may think this is a stretch, but it isn't. It is this feeling that drives some people to attempt suicide, to end it all because they feel life isn't worth living. Don't you know that this is a trick of the enemy of your soul because you have greatness in you, even though you can't see it right now?

Another sign of low self-esteem is having a "perfectionist attitude". Yup, this was me. I thought I had to be perfect in everything I did. And if I made a mistake, OMG. The world was coming to an end. I believed if I was perfect and didn't make a mistake, I would be accepted. I felt that if I did everything right, my mom wouldn't yell at me. What I missed was the fact that I was created as a fallible human being who will make mistakes on a daily basis. Justin Bieber quoted, *"I make mistakes growing. I'm not perfect; I'm not a robot."* [27] Yes, a robot.

When you are so stuck on doing everything right and afraid to make mistakes, you will restrict yourself from living and enjoying life. You will inadvertently program yourself to do, to say, to live perfectly and you will not allow yourself to be human. Now, I'm not saying go out and wow out. No, I'm saying you will stress yourself out trying to be something you are not. If you are not careful, eventually, you will burn out or up because you are applying so much pressure on yourself that you will make yourself sick. Or worse, you will slowly kill yourself. I'm telling you. It's not worth it.

Another symptom of low self-esteem is, "afraid of taking risks". This goes hand-in-hand with trying to be perfect. Taking risks is really a part of life. Going on that first date can be a risk, going to college can be a risk, joining an organization can be a risk, basically trying something new, can be a risk. Life is boring, predictable and frankly, you are n*ot living when you don't take risks. Paulo Coelho said, "Never allow waiting to become a habit. Live your dreams and take risks. Life is happening now*.[28]" This reminds me of several celebrities that started out in one industry, then made the quantum leap to another.

For example, my dude Michael Strahan. He was drafted by the NY Giants and played 14 years with them. *As a defensive end, his impressive skills earned him many awards and accolades such as a visit to the Pro Bowl 7 times, he made All-Pro 4 times and he played at the XLII Super Bowl.* (Wikipedia)[29]. When he retired in 2007, I'm sure everyone thought he would take the natural progression from football to commentating, which he did. However, he didn't stop there. He reinvented himself, took the risks and ventured into television. Today, Michael Strahan is recognized not only for his football career, but also his tenure as a co-host on, "Live with Kelly and Michael", his co-host duties on "Good Morning America" and being the host of the revamped, "$100,000 Pyramid." Most recently, he entered into a venture with JC Penney's by starting a clothing line. But, what if he had stuck to football and had not taken the risk to venture into television? Michael's influence might have been limited to just his football fans. I know a lot of women would have been very disappointed. LOL!

Another symptom of low self-esteem is not feeling worthy and thinking you don't have a voice. Many times, I have felt this way. Because my husband has been the primary breadwinner during most of our marriage, I felt as though I had no right to express how I felt about major decisions in our home. I felt that I had to go along with the program because I did not contribute on a consistent basis. Yes, I am a businesswoman and yes, I travel and speak to countless students but....when you struggle with self-esteem issues, that doesn't matter. In your mind, you see that you contribute less, you feel less, thus you are less. Even now, every so often, those feelings come back and try to stay awhile. It is then that I pump myself up and encourage myself. I have to talk myself "off of my ledge" and look at the countless contributions that I make to my family on a daily basis. But keeping it 100, there are times where the stay of "low self-esteem" is longer than I want it to be. But the plus in my life is I know I am enough. I know that any lies that "low self-esteem" tells me is just that – LIES!

Another symptom of low self-esteem is dependence - letting others make decisions, which ties into feeling as if you have no voice. When you feel as though you have no voice, you let others make decisions for you. Unfortunately, you may be viewed as weak, spineless, or wishy-washy. However, that is not the case. You are afraid to make decisions because you simply don't have confidence in your decisions. Therefore, you allow others to make the decisions for you. Unfortunately, doing so puts your life into someone else's hands, which means whatever they decide for your life is what you have to do. You have turned over your rights to someone, crowned them your God and your master, elevated them to a level higher than you and at the same time, you have demoted yourself and made yourself a “less than”. Worse yet, you feel “some kind of way” if the decision that was made was a bad decision or contrary to what you would have decided.

One last symptom I want to address. I mentioned in Chapter 2 about my struggle of trying to fit into a clique but I didn’t go into more detail, until now. As someone who struggled with low esteem and abandonment issues, like so many, I wanted to fit into the clique. The clique of the cool girls, the popular girls, people that I thought would validate me. What ended up happening was that I was bullied sexually and verbally which caused me to think that it was a mistake that I was at my new school. I felt like I was trying to fit in with people who just didn’t get me. It caused me to feel that I was trapped. All I wanted was to go back to my old school and be with the friends that I had grown up with. The friends that I could just be Lisa with. The friends that didn‘t treat me differently because I was the new girl. I felt my only way out was to end it all, just take my life. I waited until my mother wasn’t home and I took a bottle of baby aspirin and waited to die. I didn’t know that baby aspirin wouldn’t do anything but make me sick.

When my mother got home, I told her who was visibly upset. I went to school the next day and told my homeroom teacher. Instead of getting sympathy, my teacher berated me and called me a silly girl. I made a decision that I would no longer show my vulnerability to just anyone. My cry for help made me feel like a fool. That experience didn’t help the low esteem struggles that I was dealing with. In fact, it added fuel to the fire. It took years to overcome those struggles. It took me years to realize that I am enough. But, just like I now realize that I am enough, you can do the same!

Low self-esteem must be eradicated from your life, point blank, period! This crazy feeling will convince you that you are not enough. That you are worse than crap and that you are worthless, hopeless and nothing. If you do suffer from this, you have to create a self-talk that you do on a continual basis or a mantra that you say every day. My mantra is based on a profession that we used to say every Sunday at the Met which was my home church. “I am what God says I am. I can have what God says I can have. I can do what God says I can do. I can do all things through Christ who strengthens me.” You are enough! You have to keep it 100 with yourself!

WHAT ARE YOUR THOUGHTS ABOUT LOW SELF ESTEEM?

Do you suffer from low self-esteem?

What symptoms of low self-esteem do you fight?

What major opportunities have you missed because of low self-esteem?

What are your thoughts about this chapter?

How can you relate?

CHAPTER SEVEN:

DO YOU HAVE THE CONFIDENCE?

Confidence:
a feeling of trust in one's abilities, qualities, and judgment.

"Noble and great. Courageous and determined. Faithful and fearless. That is who you are and who you have always been. And understanding it can change your life, because this knowledge carries a confidence that cannot be duplicated any other way." — "Sheri L. Dew[30]

This topic can be tricky. You may think when you see a young lady walking with her head held high, rocking that hot cut with the blaring color or that guy wearing that fly outfit with Tims eloquently speaking in front of a group, he/she is confident. You may even say to yourself, "I want to be just like them." "Why can't my hair lay like hers? Or "Why can't I speak as eloquently as him?" But listen, DON'T BE FOOLED! Don't allow yourself as the observer to quietly compare or secretly covet the perceived gifts that one has. This person may be wearing a well-crafted mask that hides esteem and fear issues. They may realize that they have a job to do and the only way that they are able to get it done is to act their way through.

I remember when I first became a motivational speaker. On the outside, I was fly, I was gorgeous, I was inspiring. But on the inside, Baby, I was wondering if I was being judged. I didn't know what Lisa I should show the world. Case in point. When my husband & I hosted, "Gospel Live with DJ & Lisa", I was scared to death. Our producer, Tim Qualls, said, "girl, almost a million people are watching you." I froze. I had no confidence in myself or my abilities. Over time, I realized who better than Lisa Bryant to show up. I became confident in God, my abilities and talents and who I was. However, just like low self-esteem, lack of confidence tries to creep back into my life like an old boyfriend that won't accept the fact that we are through.

Before we go on, let's look at the definition of self-confidence. It's defined as follows: *"Self Confidence is a feeling of trust in one's abilities, qualities, and judgment."* The operative phrase in the definition is, "a feeling of trust". To be self-confident, you must have a "feeling of trust" in yourself. Now, don't get it twisted. First and foremost, before you trust yourself, you must have trust in the Lord. Trust that He will guide you and direct you. The problem with so many is there is a disconnect between their trust in God and their abilities to carry out what He says they can do. We hear, "trust God" and that sounds fine, but you must be confident that you can do what He says you can do. Thus, self-confidence is essential in pursuing the dreams and goals that you have deep in your very soul. Not to mention vital in excommunicating those life-sapping friends.

The foundation of a lack of confidence is fear. For example, you walk into a room of people you don't know. Fear tells you to stay to yourself, look down and not talk to anyone. Confidence tells you to walk into the room with your head up high, look people in their eyes and be a part of a conversation. Fear tells you not to pick up that phone to promote yourself with that potential client. Confidence tells you to not only pick up that phone but engage in a conversation and don't worry about judgment coming from the other end. Fear tells you, no one wants to hear what you have to say, that you are an imposter, that you don't know what you are talking about. Confidence tells you that you have a voice like the roar of a lion.

You see, confidence told you to apply to that college or university you are attending. Confidence told you to apply for the summer job you worked. Confidence told you to pursue a relationship with that guy, that girl that was in your Economics class or your Freshman Seminar. Don't let the fear that we talked about in Chapter Five, overshadow the confidence that you do have. That's right, you do have confidence. Fear tells you that you do not have confidence at all, that you are nothing and will never amount to anything. But confidence tells you that the two of you (you and confidence) are the real Dynamic Duo and that you are enough. You just have to keep it 100 with yourself.

Let me tell you something else about self-confidence. We all were born with confidence. As babies, we were confident that if we cried long enough, someone would feed us or change our diapers. As toddlers, we were confident that if we screamed loud enough, SOMEONE would pick us up and give us the attention that we demanded. But when did we go to the left? Where, along this journey, did we leave our confidence by the wayside? I will tell you where. On the road of untruth that whispered, "believe the lies of this world which said we had to conform to the cookie cutter images and be like everyone else". When did we trade in our childlike self-confidence for a newer, less effective and attractive model of status quo? When we allowed our creative lights to be dimmed by society and the opinions of others.

When I started my company almost four years ago, the business model was a financial services company. At the time, I was a financial professional with appointments in 4 states and I held 3 securities licenses. I thought that I wanted to help the world build their financial houses. However, deep down inside, I wanted to do workshops for Greek Letter Organizations. It was like I was leading a double life. I felt like a fraud. I talked about life insurance and annuities by day. By night, I thought about how I could make a difference in the lives of my fellow Greeks. I continued down this road for four months until my husband and I met with a guy who owned a tax preparation company. I wanted to sign a contract with him to do financial plans for his clients. He saw right through me and told me to pursue workshops with members of Greek Letter Organizations. I gained some confidence, changed the name of the company, and decided that I would change the business model to help small businesses, churches, and Greek Letter Organizations. Looking back, I see that I was all over the place with this target market, but back then, I didn't have the confidence to settle on just one.

Around the time that I changed the name of the company, I became a part of a think tank for women business owners. These awesome women would give me words of encouragement to help me in business, however, I could only partially hear them because I still didn't know who I was in business. It was during one of the mentoring sessions, that Ellyn Herbert, one of the coaches, brought to my attention that whenever I talked about the Greek Letter Organizations, I would light up and you could feel my passion. But when I talked about the churches (and this in no way diminishes my love of church or God) or small businesses, I was robotic in my responses and actions. God used her to tell me to walk in confidence and pursue my passion for helping the Greeks. I am forever grateful to Ellyn for her encouragement, Antara for her push and the other ladies that rallied around me. Yup, that was great, but I still had to walk in the confidence that this was the road that I was destined to take. It took me a minute to get there. I compared myself to these women and their successes.

What I didn't understand at the time was that my path was different. That my path into the student affairs world was way different than the Corporate America world. Comparing the two paths is just like comparing a flamingo to a peacock. Both are beautiful birds but are two totally different types of birds. Nothing is wrong with either one. However, to compare the two is senseless. I had to take the tools that I learned and apply them to my journey. When I removed the "comparison sunglasses" and sat down and thought about what I wanted my company to look like, who I wanted my company to talk to, and what message I wanted my company to proclaim, that's when things began to turn around for me. But I had to have confidence in my God-given gifts and trust my God-given vision for LM Bryant Consulting, LLC. And I had to trust that the message was relevant and that people were ready to receive it.

So, you have to ask yourself, what is a lack of confidence stopping you from pursuing? What dreams, what journey should you be on, but you are not confident that you will be accepted or taken seriously? Let me tell you something. It's time out for that. As I have said, time and time again, you are holding those gifts and talents hostage. People are waiting for you and what's inside of you. It's time to realize that the world needs the confident, handsome/beautiful butterfly that you are. You just have to walk in your God-given confidence and just step out. You must remember that you are enough. You just have to keep it 100 with yourself.

WHAT ARE YOUR THOUGHTS ABOUT CONFIDENCE?

From 1 to 10, how would you rate your confidence level?

Why?

Has a lack of confidence stopped you from pursuing your dreams?

Why do you think this is the case?

What are your thoughts about this chapter?

How can you relate?

CHAPTER EIGHT:

BE COURAGEOUS

"I Choose to Be Courageous"

Lisa Wright Bryant

"In the real world, "A Cowardly Lion" is an oxymoron".
How can a King be less than brave?
He is supposed to be a leader that is looked upon
By the weak and powerless for him to save

But now I realize that I, too, was like that lion
Shaking at the hint of uncertainty and perceived danger
I cast aside my confidence and my Divine reliance
And to courage, I became a stranger

I finally made the choice to be fearless
To embrace courage on every hand
The road to bravery has been daunting, I must confess
But the rewards of freedom have been grand."

If you know the story of the Wizard of Oz/the Wiz, the "Cowardly Lion" was afraid of ev-er-y-thing! He tried to come off as this strong, menacing animal whose roar would shake the ground. But, when this lion was challenged by Dorothy, he shrank and ran. Does that sound familiar? You come off like you are so courageous, so big and bad. But when it is time to approach your professor, your boss, your girlfriend's/your boyfriend's parents, you shrink and run. *Courageous*. Such a powerful word but what is it, and again, WHAT IS IT? According to the English Oxford Dictionary, the word, "*courageous*" is defined as, "*not deterred by danger or pain; brave*[31]."

So, before you can walk in your confidence you must be courageous enough to get up. Think of confidence as being the car and courage being the gas. Unfortunately, this is where many people have a disconnect. When you hear encouraging words, they may build your confidence which is great. However, if you are not courageous enough to fight and move past your fears, your insecurities, your past, the confidence means nothing. For example, many of you reading this book are either living on campus or in an apartment/house for the first time in your life. Initially, it was a bit challenging because this is the first time you have lived away from your parents. You must do your own laundry, pay bills, and for many of you, buy groceries. You had to be courageous and move out to live your life as a confident young adult. That is the same concept for you to living your life courageously, brave and fearlessly.

Let's look at the word, *"courage"*. This powerful word is defined as, *"the ability to do something that frightens one*".[32] Let me tell you. When I thought about leaving my first husband, I was very afraid. No, let me walk in my entire truth, I was frightened. I didn't know how to deal with people talking about me. I didn't know how to handle the people's perceptions of being a failure. I didn't want to tell my family, nor did I want to go back home. At that time, I felt like the Cowardly Lion, living the lie. But after much prayer, I mustered enough courage to leave.

Honestly, it took a minute for me to walk confidently in the fact that I made the right decision. What about you? Are you in an unhealthy relationship that you need to walk away from? If so, it's time to muster up enough courage to walk away. Now, I know I talked about this earlier, but I have learned some things need to be reiterated.

Another situation is having enough courage to ask for help when you are feeling hopeless and feel like giving up. Again, if this is not you, woohoo, that's good. But if it is you, please know that there is hope for you. There is help for you!!!!

Let me tell you something. Lack of courage tells you that you can't reach out and ask for help. Lack of courage tells you that you have to stay where you are. Lack of courage tells you that you will never be free. Lack of courage tells you that you will be victimized for the rest of your life. THAT IS SO NOT TRUE! Please ma'am, please sir, just take a step. Asking for help can make you feel at your most vulnerable. However, I am here to tell you taking that step will be one of the most courageous things you could do and it will change your life. (Side bar, be careful who you ask for help. Do your research!)

There is another situation that many of you have either faced personally, seen firsthand or have heard about, and that is hazing. At first, I was going to start this statement off with, "for you high school and college students...". However, I know some adults who have been and are being hazed OR are hazing. I want you to check this out. Below is the Delaware Hazing Law:

"CHAPTER 93. ANTI-HAZING LAW" § 9301 Short title. This chapter shall be known and may be cited as the "Anti-Hazing Law." 68 Del. Laws, c. 400, § 1.; § 9302 Definitions. The following words and phrases when used in this chapter shall have the meanings given to them in this section unless the context clearly indicates otherwise: *"Hazing" means any action or situation which recklessly or intentionally endangers the mental or physical health or safety of a student or which wilfully destroys or removes public or private property for the purpose of initiation or admission into or affiliation with, or as a condition for continued membership in, any organization operating under the sanction of or recognized as an organization by an institution of higher learning. The term shall include, but not be limited to, any brutality of a physical nature, such as whipping, beating, branding, forced calisthenics, exposure to the elements, forced consumption of any food, liquor, drug or other substance, or any other forced physical activity which could adversely affect the physical health and safety of the individual, and shall include any activity which would subject the individual to extreme mental stress, such as sleep deprivation, forced exclusion from social contact, forced conduct which could result in embarrassment, or any other forced activity which could adversely affect the mental health or dignity of the individual, or any wilful destruction or removal of public or private property. For purposes of this definition, any activity as described in this definition upon which the admission or initiation into or affiliation with or continued membership in an organization is directly or indirectly conditioned shall be presumed to be "forced" activity, the willingness of an individual to participate in such activity notwithstanding. 68 Del. Laws, c. 400, § 1.; § 9303 Hazing prohibited. Any person who causes or participates in hazing commits a class B misdemeanor. 68 Del. Laws, c. 400, § 1.; § 9304 Enforcement by institution.*

(a) Anti-hazing policy. — Each institution shall adopt a written anti-hazing policy and, pursuant to that policy, shall adopt rules prohibiting students or other persons associated with any organization operating under the sanction of or recognized as an organization by the institution from engaging in any activity which can be described as hazing. (b) Enforcement and penalties. — (1) Each institution shall provide a program for the enforcement of such rules and shall adopt appropriate penalties for violations of such rules to be administered by the person or agency at the institution responsible for the sanctioning or recognition of such organizations. (2) Such penalties may include the imposition of fines, the withholding of diplomas or transcripts pending compliance with the rules or pending payment of fines and the imposition of probation, suspension or dismissal. (3) In the case of an organization which authorizes hazing in blatant disregard of such rules, penalties may also include recision of permission for that organization to operate on campus property or to otherwise operate under the sanction or recognition of the institution. (4) All penalties imposed under the authority of this section shall be in addition to any penalty imposed for violation of paragraph (b)(3) of this section or any of the criminal laws of this State or for violation of any other institutional rule to which the violator may be subject. (5) Rules adopted pursuant hereto shall apply to acts conducted on or off campus whenever such acts are deemed to constitute hazing. 68 Del. Laws, c. 400, § 1.;[33]

The reason why I included the Delaware law for hazing is, before you become courageous enough to stand up for something, you must know what that something is. Now that you know what it is, whether it's you hazing or someone you know that is being hazed, it takes courage to say no, I will not be a part of this foolishness. I have heard so many people that attribute hazing to becoming a member of an organization. I beg to differ. Because I travel to universities across the country, I have talked to many students who have disclosed that they were hazed at summer camp or in sports. In fact, statistics state that hazing can occur in those areas and even in church groups. But, unfortunately, the ones that have stayed silent about it share a common thread, "the cowardly lion syndrome" or lack of courage to speak up and just say no. They do not speak up because they feel they do not have a voice.

Another scenario is when you know of injustices or abuses occurring and you or the person(s) affected do not speak up. It takes courage to say, "enough". It takes courage to say, "leave me alone" or "you are wrong" or even to report the incident. Unfortunately, when a person lives with the "cowardly lion syndrome," courage is not something they operate in daily. That person feels as if nothing they say or do will change the situation or circumstances. They feel as though they are voiceless and powerless. And when you feel you are lacking in so many areas, you feel as though you have no right to have a voice and power. But that train of thought is so far from the truth. As long as you have breath and pulse in your body you have a voice and power. It is that voice and that power that will allow you to speak up, push past the junk and move forward.

But you may be saying "Lisa, I AM the "Cowardly LION! I am not courageous. I am afraid of moving forward." I hear you. Trust me, I do. But that's when you must move forward. Listen, do you know what the definition of fearless is? Ariana Huffington sums it up best in her book, "On Becoming Fearless...In Love, Work, and Life". "*Fearlessness is not the absence of fear. Rather, it's the mastery of fear. Courage, my compatriot Socrates argues, is the knowledge of what is not to be feared.*[34]" When I graduated from the women's business owners group, for graduation, we all were given the bracelet that says, "fearless". I wear that bracelet when I facilitate workshops or give motivational speeches. That reminds me to have the courage and to push past the stupid conversations that sometimes occur in my head. It reminds me that I am a confident, powerful woman, blessed by God and I don't have to be concerned about the negative comments and opinions of others. Oh yes, that "fearless" bracelet is everything! Most importantly, it reminds me how courageous I am and although I started my life's journey as a statistic, because of the grace of God, I didn't stay there. See, it takes courage to leave home and go to a school where you know no one! It takes courage to put yourself out there and pursue membership in clubs and organizations. It took courage for you to graduate high school and to start the next phase of your life be it, college, military, employment, entrepreneurship, or marriage. So, give yourself some credit. Trust me, if you are reading this book, you have courage. You took a chance to purchase this book, right? Then take a chance. Take a chance former "Cowardly Lion" and pursue your dreams. You are courageous! You have courage all throughout your body! You are enough. You just have to keep it 100 with yourself!

WHAT ARE YOUR THOUGHTS ABOUT BEING COURAGEOUS?

When and where do you think you lost your childlike courage?

What do you think you should do to take back the courage you lost?

What are your thoughts about this chapter?

How can you relate?

CHAPTER NINE:

BREAKING FREE

"She decided to free herself, dance into the wind, create a new language. And birds fluttered around her, writing "yes" in the sky."[35] Monique Duval

Out of all of the quotes, this one is my new mantra. It speaks volumes to me and my personal journey called, "You Are Enough..."Writing this book, has been liberating, paralyzing, painful, numbing but most importantly, a reminder that I have been set free. This journey is like being operated on to remove a tumor, a mass that should never have been allowed to grow in the body. This journey has been like going to the salon for a trim. In order for your hair to grow and to be healthy, your stylist must get rid of the dead ends. If he/she does not, your hair will become damaged. If you do not address those dead ends, you will end up with an unwanted hairstyle because of your lack of attention to the problem.

Over the years, I have had to relive and recall incidents in my life that have been dark, painful and many times embarrassing. It has forced me to deal with some things that I thought I had dealt with, but I had not. It has stirred up many negative emotions that I thought had no longer existed BUT, I instead created a nice and cozy room for them to live out their days instead of evicting them. I had to realize that there was no need for me to be embarrassed about what was written. Instead, I made the decision to embrace my truth, the good, the bad and the ugly because it is a part of the evolution of Lisa Michele Wright Bryant. Without hurtling over those stones and boulders in the road, I would not be the woman I am today. Which leads me to breaking free.

Honestly, it has taken me decades to break free. The reason

being is because I constantly looked at my life through a negative lens. For example, if someone told me that I looked good, I would say thank you, but I would be thinking, "do you see how big these arms are?". I constantly listened to negative comments and took to heart the negative and perceived negative glances that I held close like a fur coat during a blizzard. Missed opportunities, broken dreams and chances gone is what I focused on instead of the great and wonderful things that were happening in my life. It had been that negative thinking that held me back and kept me caged for as long as I had been alive. Nevertheless, I pressed on and sought to change the trajectory of my life. I took off and destroyed the shades of negativity and decided to completely step out and pursue opportunities outside of my comfort zone. I began to dream again and follow my vision of empowering people, especially college students. I started checking myself when I heard negative comments come out of my mouth. I gave my family permission to do the same. I shut the doors to the comments and opinions of what and how people perceived Lisa should be. Instead of chasing others to find out "how they got over" and to get their autographs, I began to replay my own testimony and valued MY OWN autograph. In other words, I made the decision to become my own Shero.

Now, don't get me wrong. I do have mentors that I talk to and bounce ideas off them. However, I don't place their words over what Jesus did for me. Speaking of Jesus, He is the reason why I am free. I tell you, if I were Him, I would have left me a long time ago. My reason? Because He told me I was free, gave me the blueprints for success and told me He would be with me and to just go get it. Of course, I did the opposite. But once I accepted the truth that I was enough, I was able to break free!!!!! Ain't no stopping me now, Baby!

Did you hear what I said, "once I accepted the truth that I was enough"? There it is. The solution to the mystery. To break free, you have to accept the truth that you are enough and there is nothing else in this world that could complete you. Absolutely nothing. The word "enough" is defined as, "as much or as many as required". The definition of the word is self-explanatory. This simply means "*as much*". So, let's look up that word in the context of the title of this book. You are enough. Let's look at it again: you all are enough! That statement alone should be one of liberty, one of freedom, one that releases you from the chains and the bondage that go along with "I'm not enough". That statement should be one that frees you from asking yourself, what do I have to do to be whole? Why? Because you are whole! Even if you have flaws, you are still enough!!! That statement alone should be one that liberates you from the thought that a man or a woman is necessary to make you enough. Nothing in this world was designed and created to complete you. Those people, those things were designed and created to enhance you, not to make you whole. You are already whole!!! Oh no, my sister! Please, my brother! If you think that is not you, then this book was written with you in mind.

So, what comes to mind when you hear that You, yes you, are enough? Do you believe that? Do you believe that when God created you in His image, He created you as a complete person? If you believe it, wonderful. Continue to do so. But if you don't, today is the day to make a decision that you will no longer think less of yourself. No longer will you think that you are not good enough. No longer will you think that you are incapable of doing anything right. Today is the day that you will adopt the mantra, "I am enough!"

Once you realize that you are enough, you will break free from the pains and heartaches of the past that have held you back for so long. Once you realize that you are enough, you will break free from allowing the opinions of people to paralyze you. Once you realize that you are enough, you will break free from comparing yourself with your perception of others. By the way, at the end of the day, you really don't know those people anyway, do you? Once you realize that you are enough, you will break free from F.E.A.R. and its damaging effects on your life. Once you realize that you are enough, you will break free from thinking you are a less than and will dismiss low self-esteem. Once you realize that you are enough, you will walk with confidence. Once you realize that you are enough, you will infuse yourself with courage, like you are giving yourself a blood transfusion. You see, this battle of knowing whether or not you are enough doesn't start with anyone else but you. It starts in your mind. You must divorce yourself from the negativity that has bound some of you for years, decades. You must make up in your mind TODAY that you will no longer accept those stumbling blocks that have thwarted many of your plans, your steps into a better life.

Now here's the thing. The journey to breaking free does not stop there. First, you accept the fact that you are enough, then you must walk in it. How do you do it? By doing a mind reset. Whenever an app on your electronic device acts a little crazy, you have to clear the data and cache. For your device, you go to the 'Home' screen, then Settings > Applications > Manage Applications >then the crazy app. Once you clear your data and cache, turn your device off, then back on again and let it reboot. So, for you, it's time to clear the data and cache. How do you do this? By making some external variations to bring about internal changes. What outward changes?

You may have to change who you hang with. You may have to issue articles of divorce to some of those friends who are keeping you in a world that allows you to be a subset of your true self. As I mentioned earlier in this book, if you are trying to make a change and you keep those ratchet friends, you will never experience a genuine breakthrough. You may have to change what you are doing for entertainment. If you are someone who enjoys pornography (videos, pictures, texts, movies) I would strongly suggest replacing it with other types of videos, pictures, texts, and movies. Studies show that pornography gives the viewer a distorted, unrealistic view of sex and intimacy. It could also cause the viewer to develop an unhealthy body image because they compare themselves to the bodies of the actors in those movies.

Another external change is shifting your surroundings. You might have to move or evict your roommate(s). You would be surprised how much better you feel when you have peace, at the time you walk into your dorm room or apartment and you are not met with mayhem and foolishness. Trust me. There's nothing like peace of mind. Other changes are joining a support group, working out (yes, studies prove that endorphins are released when you work out), journaling (hint, hint) and starting your day reciting motivational and inspirational poems or quotes.

One last external change is developing a prayer life and seeking God for deliverance and peace. I am a firm believer that positive change cannot come without him. When you go to the Lord in prayer, you can do a strength exchange. You give him the crap and He will give you peace.

Some of you may have to seek professional help because those stumbling blocks have become boulders and not you, not your circle of friends, not your family are equipped or trained to help you process and get rid of the baggage that you have accumulated. And guess what? It's all Gucci! Whatever it legally takes for you to walk in your freedom. Some of you may have to sit down with some family members about things that have happened in your past. Whatever course of action is required, the time is now to take it. It's time out for allowing life to pass you by while you barely exist, marching in place paralyzed, because of the yoke about your neck and the chains about your ankles. The sad part is, although you are young, many of you have been paralyzed in the same place for 3, 5, or 10 years.

So, ask yourself this question: don't you think it's time to no longer "be about that life" and be your best self, living a life that is truly lit, beyond measure? Don't you think it's time to stop allowing yourself to be robbed of your youth by negative thought patterns, friends, and family that have held your life in their hands for far too long? Aren't you tired of being the star of someone else's puppet show, manipulated and forced to entertain them AND their people at their beckoned call? Aren't you tired of acting like you are happy for everyone else and not for yourself? Aren't you just sick and tired of being sick and tired? Then it's time to declare war. Declare war on those links that have formed a chained noose around your neck and shackles around your feet. Use that negativity as a huge rock to break those chains and shackles! It's time to break free! It's time to break free! It's time to break free! It's time to declare. I AM ENOUGH! TIME TO KEEP IT 100 WITH MYSELF!

WHAT ARE YOUR THOUGHTS ABOUT BREAKING FREE?

List the things that you have allowed that has stopped you from breaking free.

How are you going to stop them from stopping you?

What are your thoughts about this chapter?

How can you relate?

CHAPTER TEN:

"FOLLOWING YOUR DREAMS"

Consult not your fears but your hopes and your dreams. Think not about your frustrations, but about your unfulfilled potential. Concern yourself not with what you tried and failed in, but with what it is still possible for you to do. Pope John XXIII[36]

Throughout this book, you have gotten words of wisdom, encouragement and my personal testimony detailing the challenges that can potentially stop you from moving forward and following your dreams. In the previous chapter, I challenged you to use that negativity, those negative situations as a boulder to break the chains round about you. It is at that time, you can truly pursue your dreams with abandon. When you are no longer concerned about how you look to others or their opinions, that's when you can follow your dreams. Those God-given dreams were placed into you when you were still in your mother's womb. Your experiences, good, bad and ugly, were allowed to serve as fertilizer to those dreams, which one day would lead you to your destiny. Those dreams were placed in you to change the world and to empower a generation. Those dreams were not meant to die with you. Oh no. Those dreams were placed in you to come alive at an appointed time, to be shared, and to show the world how great God is and how awesome you are.

Writing this book is a dream come true for me. There will be many more books to come from me so keep your eyes and ears open. It has been without question a journey for me. When I finally said "yes" I would write this book, my world turned upside down with the death of my beloved father-in-love, Sammie B and the cancer diagnosis of my mommy, G$. But I persevered. Many days, I sat at my computer typing and crying because several of the things detailed in this book, I had not thought about in many years.

There were days I had to walk after writing and there were days I had to walk away from the book, sometimes for weeks. BUT, I had to make the decision that I must follow my dreams of empowering a nation. Yes, I travel and speak, teach and preach but what if someone cannot make the event I am speaking at. Shouldn't they be empowered too? That is why this book is important. It is meant to help others be their best selves and be honest with themselves.

You see, I too had to break some chains in this process. I even had to have conversations with some family members and friends to get free, so I could follow my dreams of becoming an author that empowers others.

So where am I now? I am realizing some of my dreams, and patiently waiting for the others to manifest. My number one dream has come true. I have always, always, always wanted to be a wife and mother. There were several times in my life when it looked like it would never happen. But now, I have a wonderful husband whom I love, honor and respect, three beautiful children, one by love, two by blood, and 2 amazing grandchildren. On top of that, Jesus honored me to have countless children whose DNA I don't share.

Another dream was for me to go to West Chester State College/ West Chester University just like my music teacher, Barbara "Bobbie" Malone Mina. I love that woman! She was my role model at Toby Farms Elementary School. She imparted so much into me and taught me what a caring music teacher looked like. She also taught me how to play the flutophone and piano. I almost missed out on attending West Chester because of fear. I waited until their very last audition date in June, one week before my high school graduation, because I was so afraid of the audition. But, I overcame it and performed an 11-page piece from memory. I made a mistake during the audition and I just knew that my dreams of attending West Chester were over. A week later, my dream was realized when I was accepted into the performance program. Years later, I decided to run for the West Chester University Alumni Association Board of Directors to give back to my beloved Alma Mater. Again, fear almost stopped me. I submitted my application the first year and was declined. But this time, instead of giving into fear, I applied again and was accepted. I was voted in by my fellow alums and the rest is history.

To conclude, I have been blessed. In spite of every opportunity that I have blocked, the fear issues, the lack of self-confidence, the self-inflicting mental abuse, God has been good to me. Finally, I realized that I am enough. In spite of my flaws, I am enough. I also now believe the sky is the limit for me. I also know now that I have a great work to do. I must let everyone I meet know that no matter what they face, they are powerful beyond measure. I must show them that instead of running from their issues, they must face them and let them know that they have the upper hand.

So, for all of you in the process of breaking free and pursuing your dreams, I will leave you with one of my favorite quotes from the Matrix. Morpheus knew that Neo was "the one", but Neo did not believe he was, let alone confident to walk in that position. After his training, Neo was still afraid, still unsure of himself and who he was. It was then he asked Morpheus, *"What are you trying to tell me? That I can dodge bullets?" Morpheus responded, "No, Neo. I'm trying to tell you that when you're ready, you won't have to."*[37] I'm telling you today, when you walk free of the bondage of not knowing who you are and walking in the confidence that you are enough, you will be able to accomplish great exploits and pursue your dreams. You won't have to dodge that negative bullet anymore. That bullet will now have to dodge you. Remember, you are enough. Keep it 100 with yourself!

FOLLOWING YOUR DREAMS

What dreams do you want to accomplish within the next 5 years?

How are you going to accomplish bringing your dreams into fruition?

What are your thoughts about this chapter?

How can you relate?

How has this journey changed your life?

EPILOGUE

There is only one me. That means NO one else can do the things I do like me. I don't have to compare myself to others nor exert all my energy to squeeze myself into a clique that does not appreciate my uniqueness. I am happy with who I am and who I am becoming. I am great, I am powerful, I am anointed and appointed by God to do things no one else was or ever will be created to do. I don't have to accept anything less than what Jesus has for me. I don't have to allow everyone to take residence in my galaxy. I am beautiful and free as a Monarch butterfly. I will take other people's opinions into consideration when it lines up with the will of God for my life. I will no longer compare myself with others and where they are on this journey called life. Instead, I will cheer them on as I continue to finish the countless assignments I was created to complete. Lastly, I will walk in the truth that I am Enough. When I was born, I was enough. Growing up, I was enough. As an adult, I am enough. When I leave this earth and join my Savior, I will still be enough. I am enough. And I will keep it 100 with myself!

Lisa Wright Bryant

REFERENCES

1. Act 1, Scene III of the famous play, “Hamlet”, spoken by Polonius
2. https://www.biography.com/news/nelson-mandelas-birthday-and-biography-a-timeline-of-events-20881773
3. http://smallbusiness.chron.com/truth-advertisements-airbrushing-34031.html
4. http://www.telegraph.co.uk/news/politics/liberal-democrats/6516537/Airbrushed-images-harming-girls-and-boys-experts-say.html
5. http://www.dictionary.com/browse/jealous
6. https://www.brainyquote.com/quotes/quotes/h/heidiklum449843.html
7. https://www.vocabulary.com/dictionary/formative
8. https://www.psychologytoday.com/blog/the-new-resilience/201310/why-the-impact-child-abuse-extends-well-adulthood
9. https://en.wikipedia.org/wiki/Peer_pressure
10. Shannon Thomas southlakecounseling.org
11. https://www.goodreads.com/quotes/5245-i-can-t-give-you-a-sure-fire-formula-for-success-but
12. https://www.brainyquote.com/quotes/quotes/s/stevejobs416854.html
13. Reference from “What’s Love Got to Do With It”
14. I Kings 18:21
15. Sheryl Brady, “Say It Loud, Say It Clear” sermon
16. Max Ehrmann, "Desiderata", The Poems of Max Ehrmann (1948)
17. http://www.fitstream.com/articles/stop-comparing-yourself-to-others-a212
18. https://www.goodreads.com/quotes/976049-f-e-a-r-has-two-meanings-forget-everything-and-run-or-face

19. http://www.biblestudy.org/bibleref/meaning-of-numbers-in-bible/18.html
20. Oxford Dictionary
21. https://www.merriam-webster.com/dictionary/fear
22. https://www.brainyquote.com/quotes/quotes/e/eleanorroo121157.html
23. https://www.brainyquote.com/quotes/oprah_winfrey_121366?src=t_failure
24. Anonymous
25. https://www.ucdmc.ucdavis.edu/hr/hrdepts/asap/Documents/Self_esteem.pdf
26. "Brain Drain the Breakthrough That Will Change Your Life"
27. Taken from Justin Bieber's interview with Ryan Seacrest
28. Paulo Coelho http://www.paulocoelhoblog.com/
29. https://en.wikipedia.org/wiki/Michael_Strahan
30. https://www.codeofliving.com/quotes/27-powerful-quotes-boost-your-self-confidence
31. https://en.oxforddictionaries.com/definition/courageous
32. https://en.oxforddictionaries.com/definition/courage
33. http://delcode.delaware.gov/title14/c093/index.shtml
34. https://www.huffingtonpost.com/2012/05/02/what-it-means-to-be-fearless_n_1457118.html
35. https://www.goodreads.com/quotes/601277-she-decided-to-free-herself-dance-into-the-wind-create
36. https://www.brainyquote.com/quotes/quotes/p/popejohnxx109443.html
37. http://www.imdb.com/character/ch0000741/quotes

Made in the USA
Middletown, DE
27 March 2019